# COMPLETE KARATE

# COMPLETE KARATE

## J. Allen Queen

 Sterling Publishing Co., Inc.  New York

Edited by Claire Bazinet
Photographs by Samuel Jones III
Drawings by Patsy Queen

**Library of Congress Cataloging-in-Publication Data**

Queen, J. Allen.
    Complete karate / J. Allen Queen.
      p.  cm.
    Includes index.
    Summary: Introduces the art and sport of karate, covering
stances, punches, kicks, blocks, counters, and the performance of two katas,
or karate forms.
    ISBN 0-8069-8678-6
    1. Karate—Juvenile literature.  [1. Karate.]  I. Title.
GV1114.32.Q44   1993
796.8′ 153—dc20                          93-24831
                                                 CIP
                                                 AC

10  9  8  7  6  5  4  3  2  1

First paperback edition published in 1994 by
Sterling Publishing Company, Inc.
387 Park Avenue South, New York, N.Y. 10016
© 1993 by J. Allen Queen
Distributed in Canada by Sterling Publishing
% Canadian Manda Group, P.O. Box 920, Station U
Toronto, Ontario, Canada M8Z 5P9
Distributed in Great Britain and Europe by Cassell PLC
Villiers House, 41/47 Strand, London WC2N 5JE, England
Distributed in Australia by Capricorn Link (Australia) Pty Ltd.
P.O. Box 6651, Baulkham Hills, Business Centre, NSW 2153, Australia
*Manufactured in the United States of America*
*All rights reserved*

Sterling ISBN 0-8069-8678-6 Trade
                 0-8069-8679-4 Paper

*In memory of*
*Kellie Jones Harris*
*and*
*Cynthia Caroline Harper*

# Introducing Karate

Welcome to the exciting art and sport of karate. By learning the techniques of karate, you can begin to gain greater self-confidence, improve your overall athletic ability, and be able to defend yourself against any attacker of any size.

Most of the ideas that you have about karate and the other martial arts from the Orient may be limited to what you have seen on television or in the movies. In those productions, you may have seen karate masters leaping through the air, kicking bad guys and saving the day. What you have seen does have some karate elements but gymnastics and trick photography are thrown in. What you will learn in this book is the true art and sport of karate. Are you ready to begin? If so, let's start by looking at the history of karate.

## The History of Karate

Karate began in the Orient over two thousand years ago. Many karate masters of today believe that monks living in secluded monasteries watched the movement of animals on the attack or fighting and practised these movements until these new fighting skills were mastered. One interesting tale is a story of a great monk who travelled over the Himalayan Mountains from India into China to serve as a master in a newly formed monastery. When he arrived he found his soon-to-be followers in superior mental states but physically weak. He immediately required that his students balance their daily meditations with physical exercise. The great master was wise in that he had his students observe animals in combat. He guided his students to be powerful and aggressive like the big cats and to strike quickly like the snake. Even the mythical dragon was brought to life as students were taught to kick, like the dragon whipping his giant tail. Insects were watched also for what they could teach. Probably the most notable was the praying mantis, considered to be a great fighter. Since the great master's students had already learned high-level mental control through years of meditation, the addition of the newly gained physical skills became a new art form which could be used for both self-defense and self-discipline.

No one knows for sure if the above story is true or a myth. However, if you were to watch some of the great Kung Fu masters demonstrate their art, you would see the cat, the dragon, the praying mantis, and other animals in their movements. If this is truly the way modern-day karate began, you can see why karate is an art form which shows respect to all creatures and is a highly disciplined art. Even if the story is false, the early masters used great imagination as they developed karate. Their purpose was to create a balance between the mental and physical abilities of their followers. They probably didn't intend to develop a fighting art. Yet, many believe that this is how the art form of Kung Fu began and most martial arts' scholars agree that Kung Fu is the father of modern-day karate.

Karate first began in China and over many years continued to develop and spread to other countries. In China many forms of Kung Fu developed over hundreds of years. Some students specialized in either the Crane, Snake, or Tiger forms. Over centuries many of these true forms changed into modern styles of Kung Fu, such as Wing Chung that Bruce Lee initially studied. Not all Kung Fu styles are designed for defense. Today you can find old and young alike practising a form of exercise called Tai Chi Chuan. In fact, there are many types of Tai Chi practised. It takes many years to master Tai Chi Chuan, just as it takes many years to master the art of karate.

It is not known how Kung Fu and other forms of self-defense spread to other countries in the Orient but it is believed that, as Kung Fu spread, much adaptation was done to the art. As a result karate was born. Since the adaptations or changes took different forms, you can now find many types of karate. The major systems of karate today come from the countries of Korea, Japan, and Okinawa. The different systems are similar with some variations in stances, kicks, and blocks. The variations are most evident in the forms of the karate "dances" known as kata (kah-tuh).

Today, in Korea, you can find several different styles of karate. Korean karate, known as Tae Kwon Do, is taught all over the world. While there are more similarities than differences found in the many styles of karate, the differences are very obvious. For example, if you were to watch a student of Korean karate and a student of Japanese karate you would still see many similarities. However, you would also see some differences. Why? The Japanese people tended to be shorter than the Koreans. In Japanese karate you would notice a greater emphasis on hand techniques, while in Korean karate, you would see more emphasis placed on kicks. The Korean student using more kicks in his sparring while the Japanese student using more punches appear to be adaptations because of height. Most of Japanese karate came from Okinawa. Master Funakoshi from Okinawa introduced karate to the Japanese royalty in the early 1900s. He remained in Japan and further developed his famous style of karate known as Shotokan (*show-toe-kon*). Funakoshi is honored as the "Father of Japanese Karate." Other great masters of the 1920s and 1930s developed other Japanese styles of karate. One great teacher, Master Mabuni, was the founder of Shito-ryu (*she-toe-roo*) karate. Shito-ryu is one of the most popular styles of karate in Japan. It is the style of karate that you will learn in this book.

Karate has now become a popular sport all over the world. Karate was introduced to the United States right after World War II, in the late 1940s. By the 1980s you could find karate schools in most towns and cities in every state. A karate tournament can be found every week of the year somewhere in the United States. In fact, most weeks you will have many tournaments from which to choose.

While many of the Oriental styles of karate still exist today, you will find several instructors teaching the best aspects of several different styles. Many different styles of American karate have been developed and these karate schools can be found throughout the United States. While many of these schools are quite good, many instructors have removed the Oriental traditions and rituals that have long

played an important part in the proper development of a well-rounded karate student.

In the past ten years there have been several efforts to combine the many styles of karate into one system or organization, like that found in the art of judo. Judo, an art from Japan which uses throws and pinning techniques, has only one style and it has been in the Olympics for years. Karate has only recently appeared in the Olympics. Its future as an Olympic event is questionable.

## The Study of Karate

Karate is literally translated as "empty

hands'' since no weapons other than parts of the body are used. Today, karate is studied by thousands of children and adults. Over eighty-five percent of karate students are male. Most of the boys are between the ages of nine and twelve. This is unfortunate since girls who study karate do extremely well and usually have better form than boys at the earlier ages. Adults of any age can practise karate. However, it is unusual to find adults practising karate past the age of forty-five. Master Funakoshi studied and taught karate into his eighties.

Unlike team sports, karate teaches you to depend upon your own individual skills and gives you the chance to use your physical and mental skills for self-defense. Like many individual sports, karate is also a sport which allows you to enter tournaments and win trophies and awards.

The movements and techniques you learn in karate are quite graceful and beautiful. Some aspects look like boxing while other parts of karate resemble a dance or ballet. You will find karate challenging, but fun. You can practise karate by yourself, with a partner, or in a class.

To do karate, you combine leg, arm, and body movements into a system for self-defense. In the beginning, until you master control of all of your kicks and punches, you don't actually hit anyone while you practise karate. You learn to stop your punches and kicks before you touch your partner's body. This is the way you learn to gain full control of your kicks and punches. Later, you will have the skills to make "light contact" to your sparring partner or opponent. You would only strike a person with "full contact" if he or she attacks you or tries to hurt you. Karate students can learn to disable, maim, or even kill an attacker with lightning speed and accuracy. However, it is very important for you to know that this is not the major goal of karate. Karate is an art form and a sport. Karate masters know how to avoid unsafe situations and use their heads, not their fists, to solve problems. You should never strike an individual with full force unless you are in a life-threatening situation.

## Karate and Self-Esteem

Your body and mind are always developing as you grow. You learn that you need friends, family, and fun recreation to be happy and to grow in a healthy manner. Your activities at home, school, and in the community all influence your mental and physical growth. Most educators agree that a sport or hobby which gives you a chance to think and to focus your physical skills is good for you.

As you learn karate, you will become more self-confident and more independent. You will enjoy doing things for yourself. In addition to improved physical fitness, you will be able to think and perform better in school and in all other activities in which you are involved. Most importantly, you will learn self-discipline and

responsibility, and how to control your anger and fear. Do you know how good you feel about yourself when you win a race or hit a home run? That good feeling is self-esteem. Self-esteem is how you value or feel about yourself. Successful athletes, scholars, and winners of all types have positive self-esteem. Learning karate is an excellent way to gain self-esteem. As you grow as a karate student, you will see

growth in other aspects of your life. Karate students are well mannered, strive for high academic performance in school, and have a sense of self-assurance and control that is admired by peers.

It is important here to state that you should never play around, showing off what you learn in karate. One reason not to do this is that someone may get hurt. Another reason is that people do not like show-offs. You might lose the respect of your friends if you are perceived as bragging or boasting of your knowledge of karate. The true karate student, or karateka, only practices karate at home, in class, or in a tournament.

## Learning Karate

The three words that best describe what you must do in order to learn and become good in karate are practise, practise, and practise. No kidding! Just as in acquiring any new skill, such as playing the piano, running a sprint, or drawing a picture, the more you practise—actually *do* it—the better and faster you will learn or improve the skill. This is true in karate. Practice is most important.

One of the first rules of learning karate is safety. Never do anything that will hurt you or anyone else. Getting a medical checkup is the first step. Unfortunately, as with any sport, accidental injury is always possible. In order to minimize the risk of any accidental injury, it is always important to be careful in all aspects of karate practice. As explained previously, you never actually hit another person. You would only strike another person in self-defense, if you were physically attacked and your life was in danger. As you continue to study the art of karate, you will learn how to deliver a crippling or deadly blow if necessary to defend yourself.

## Nutrition and Karate

You need to eat foods that are good for your body and help you to grow. Foods rich in complex carbohydrates will give you the energy you need to practise hard and for long periods of time. Complex carbohydrates can be found in such foods as rice, potatoes, corn, and other vegetables. Apples and bananas are also good sources.

Drink plenty of low-fat milk for calcium and eat healthful proteins found in lean beef, chicken, and fish to keep your muscles and bones growing strong. Breads, cereals, and grains are good sources of Vitamin B, which will keep your body functioning well. Fresh fruits and juices are good sources of Vitamin C, which will help defend your body against germs and diseases. Remember to drink plenty of water to replace what you lose during hard workouts. Ask your health teacher or doctor about specific nutritional needs based upon your age, size, and weight.

# How to Become a Karate Champion

Every karate student is a winner. Not everyone can become a champion or karate master but everyone wins. You win because you learn to improve your physical skills and your mental well-being. However, every champion knows that there are three ingredients in the recipe for winning:

**1.** *Positive Attitude* Be positive about all aspects of your life including school, home, and community. Look at your karate practice as a vehicle for improving your life. Develop strong values and healthy habits. Avoid things that will hurt you.

**2.** *Mental Discipline* How you view the world and how you think can strongly influence your physical skills. Mental discipline will give you the control to be a winner. You will improve your concentration, which will increase your mental and physical focus, and thus improve your karate skills. You will be more dedicated to mastering each skill. When in competition, mental discipline will keep you focused and on target. You will be able to control your anger in the most stressful situations.

**3.** *Physical Fitness* Physical fitness is obviously important in karate. By practising the exercises found in this book, you will improve the karate skills you learn and become a winner.

Therefore, the formula for winning is positive attitude + mental discipline + physical fitness.

To become a karate champion or to master the art, you will have to work under the guidance of a qualified karate master, but you can learn the major skills and karate techniques from this book. Later, you will need an instructor in order to move on to the more advanced levels. Although a karate instructor can help you improve your skills as you develop, the cost of karate instruction prevents many young people from enrolling in a karate school. You may want to learn everything you can from this book and evaluate your progress. If you are progressing well and you have learned to execute all of the skills found in this book, you may then want to seek out an instructor. Most instructors charge anywhere from $50 to $80 a month for two or three lessons per week. Other instructors require large sums of money even to begin the class. Avoid the expensive classes. Many of these instructors are into karate more for the money than for bringing more students into the art of karate.

Many instructors will not accept you into their classes if you are under ten years old. Even worse, some instructors will not give you good individual guidance. Before you join a class or sign up for lessons, ask present karate students how they like their instructor. What are his or her qualifications? Maybe you can be allowed to sit in on one class before you decide.

An instructor may be excellent for adults, but may not know how to teach *you* in the best way. Young people need more time to learn each karate skill. You may not be able to master some karate skills as quickly or as easily because of your size or age. The instructor may not explain things to you as clearly as your teacher at school does. More importantly, the instructor may not have the skill or the patience to teach karate to children.

A karate instructor should have at least a first-degree black belt and like working with students your age. The ideal instructor should have experience as a school teacher or experience and knowledge about childhood growth and development. He should have a sincere interest in young children. In choosing an instructor, follow these three pointers:

**1.** *Find a helpful and patient instructor.* Don't get one who screams or hits students when they make mistakes. You learn from mistakes and you will make plenty in the beginning—everyone does. You need someone who is understanding and makes you feel comfortable.

**2.** *Take a class with people your own age.* You will get confused learning karate with adults. They are bigger and their muscles are stronger and better developed than yours. Adult classes move too quickly for young people.

**3.** *Promotion to the next rank should be based on your ability.* Many instructors, unfortunately, promote students based on their success in karate tournaments. You should be judged on your ability and not on whether or not you win in a tournament. In fact, many students never enter karate tournaments. Some of the greatest karate masters in history, men and women, were never in a tournament.

## Dressing for Karate

To begin practising karate, all you really need is a pair of loose pants and a sweat shirt. You will, however, need a karate suit, or gi (*gee*), to enter a tournament (**1**). Karate suits come in a variety of sizes, colors, and styles. The traditional suit is the most common. It usually comes in either white (**2**) or black. Some students choose to mix colors by wearing pants a different color than the jacket (**3**). You can add colored stripes to the suit (**4**) or various patterns such as stars and stripes (**5**). Some students like to add a patch that represents their karate club or karate style (**6**). As you progress in karate, you may like a more colorful or flashy suit (**7**). These suits are made of satinlike material, but much

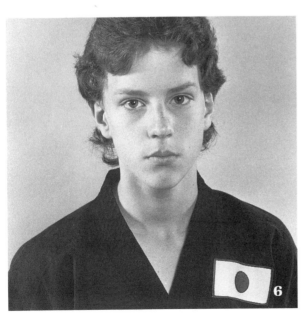

stronger. If you can sew, or someone has offered to make you a karate suit, patterns, just like commercial suits, can be ordered from companies that advertise in karate magazines. Suits come in sizes from triple zero for toddlers and preschoolers (1) (al- though you will not see many very young children under six actually learning kara- te) through size seven, which is for large adults over six feet tall. Suits come in many colors. The more traditional suits have drawstring pants (2) and wrap-around

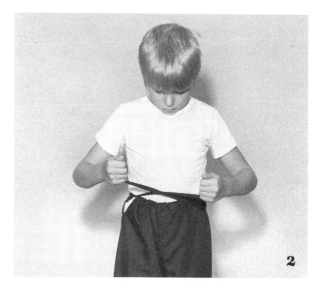

jackets **(3)**. Non-traditional suits come with lace-up pants or elastic waistband pants. Some suits come with a short sport-style jacket **(4)**.

**4**

**Tieing the Belt**

**Step 1** Fold the belt in half in front of you to find the middle. Hold the two ends in your left hand and the folded middle in your right (**1**).

**Step 2** Open the belt and line up the middle of it across your waist (**2**).

Although an authentic karate suit will give you a greater sense of being a karate student, a suit is not necessary. But if you do have a suit, you will need to know how to tie the belt properly.

**Step 3** Wrap both ends behind your back and bring them around to the front again (**3**).

**Step 4** Pull the left end up between your jacket and belt at your waist (**4**).

**Step 5** Cross the right end over and then under the left end (**5**).

**Step 6** Tie the belt tightly into a knot (**6**) and let the two ends fall in front of your gi (**7**).

When the belt is tied correctly, both of the ends are the same length (**8**).

If you order a suit, be sure to get a white belt to make your suit complete. As a beginner, you will wear the white belt. When you improve your skills over the next few years, your rank will increase to yellow, orange, green, blue, brown, and then black. Generally, the darker the belt, the higher the rank. With few exceptions, you will be matched with students of the same rank when you enter a tournament.

In addition to the belt, you will need headgear plus hand and foot gloves (1) and a mouth guard (2). Boys are required to wear a cup athletic supporter. Some boys and girls also like to wear shin pads and elbow pads (3).

In addition to a karate suit or a sweatsuit, you will need a workout space. You need an area that will allow you to do all of the warmup exercises and karate kicks and punches. Usually a large room or part of the garage is quite adequate. In nice weather, the patio or backyard works well (4).

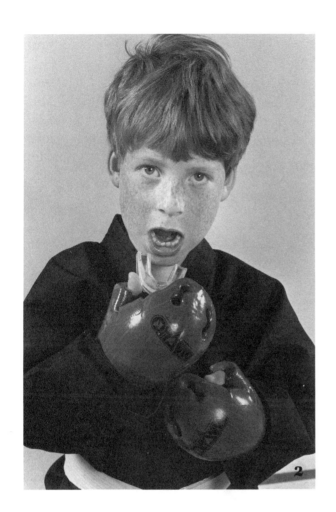

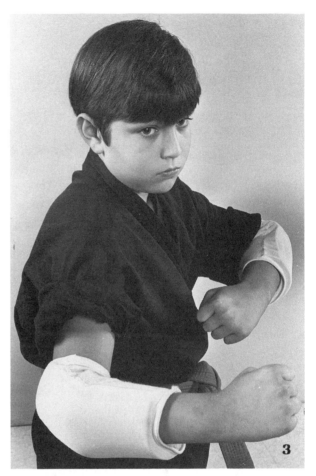

## Are You Ready?

Before you begin the study of karate, talk with your parents about your interest in karate. Ask them for their support and guidance. If your parents are able, ask them to study karate with you.

Remember to always show respect for the art of karate. Never strike another individual (except in self-defense). Never brag about karate or demonstrate your skills to other boys and girls, or lose your temper and strike out. Always be in control and learn to focus your kicks, punches, and strikes within one inch of the target without hitting. If you agree with this philosophy, you are now ready to begin. Good luck, be careful, and have fun.

# Starting the Workout

## Meditation

Starting from your first workout, perform the meditation ritual. Meditation is used to clear your mind before and after karate practice. It has nothing to do with religion.

Meditation can help you get in the right frame of mind for practice. Meditation can also be practised right before a big game or exam. This will help you be more focused and in control. Many people use meditation to control stress and feel better.

A good exercise to help you in your meditation practice is to focus on one object, such as the flame of a candle (with your parents' guidance and permission first—for safety reasons), a light reflected in a mirror, or a spot on the wall. Focus hard into the object and think of nothing else. If you find yourself thinking of anything else focus harder. This is an excellent exercise to clear your mind and lower your stress level. Your parents may want to try this technique to relax. If you get where you can focus for five or six minutes at a time, you will do an excellent job when you meditate in karate.

To meditate in karate, first get into the position. Kneel down and place the tops of your toes and feet flat on the floor. Then sit back on your heels. Close your eyes and focus mentally on what you are going to do during this practice. Visualize yourself throwing the perfect kick or punch. To have this in your mind will help you physically arrive at perfection with the kick or punch.

You meditate at the beginning and at the end of every karate practice. Do not leave this element of karate study out of your routine. Many of the great masters would meditate for hours visualizing perfect form before physical practice.

## The Bow

It is important to learn to do the bow, which is used before and after karate class

or before and after sparring with an opponent (**1**). To bow properly, first stand erect with your hands at your sides and your feet together or slightly apart (**2**). Then, with a stiff and slow movement, bend forward at the waist and return to the erect position (**3**).

In addition to bowing to your instructor in class or sparring in a kumite (*koo-muh-tay*) match (**4**), you bow at the beginning and ending of a kata (**5**), a series of prearranged moves that start simple and become more complex as you advance in rank.

Some instructors require students to bow before and on entering the workout studio or dojo (*doe-joe*) **(6)**. You may want to do the same as you begin your workout at home. The bow is always done to show respect for your instructors **(7)**, judges, partners, and tournament opponents. It is also done to show respect to yourself, which is of great importance.

## Warm-up Exercises

Any great athlete knows the importance of warming up before a match or game. Go to a basketball game or a tennis match and watch the players do a series of exercises before play starts. Just as meditation will get you ready mentally for practice, exercises will get you ready physically. Get into the habit of exercising before practice. Your muscles can be easily hurt without proper warm-up exercises. Do the basic movements described in this chapter to warm up your body for a karate workout. Stretching is the most important activity. It makes you more flexible. You will need great flexibility to be successful in karate.

As you do these exercises, begin slowly. Gradually increase your movement. Exercise should never be painful. It is a good idea for you to have a checkup by your doctor before beginning any exercise program. This is especially true if you have not been physically active, are overweight, or if you have a special problem.

The four elements you want to work for in your exercises are to gain balance, flexibility, speed, and power. Balance and flexibility will be gained by concentrated practice. Speed and power will grow with repetition of practice.

Complete these exercises daily before beginning karate practice. You should also do a few stretches slowly after your workout as a cool-down activity. This is as important as doing warm-up exercises. Don't forget!

For the most part, these exercise should be done in the order given. The order is designed to warm up certain muscle groups in the proper sequence. Basically, you will begin at the top of your body and work downward. The first exercise is the neck roll.

## Neck Roll

This exercise loosens and strengthens the neck muscles. The neck muscles can be easily pulled when you are working out or in a match. Unfortunately, many sports enthusiasts never bother to warm up the neck area. This could be a costly mistake because it is an easy area to damage.

Stand with your feet shoulder-width apart and tip your head to the left (**1**). Now, slowly roll your head rearward (**2**) and then move it to the right (**3**). Throughout the exercise, focus on the neck muscles and do the roll slowly. Return your head to the beginning position. Complete the entire circle five times. Increase the amount with practice until you can do twelve complete circles comfortably. If

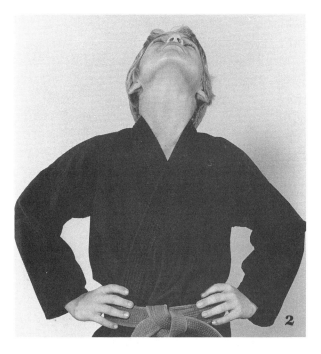

you feel dizzy at all, you are doing the rolls too fast.

After you complete the neck exercise, rest for a minute and begin the single arm rotation exercise.

## Single Arm Rotation

This exercise loosens your shoulder and arm muscles. Since you have loosened the neck area it is now time to move down the body. You will be using your arms and shoulders in all aspects of karate. It is important to spend several minutes getting these areas ready for the workout. Start slowly and increase your speed as you warm up.

To begin, stand straight with your feet shoulder-width apart and swing your left arm forward (**1**). Next, swing your arm upwards (**2**). Now, swing your arm behind you as if you were winding a large clock. Finish with your arm at your side (**3**). Do ten complete circles with your left arm and then ten complete circles with your right arm. Increase your speed when you

reach the sixth rotation. To further loosen these muscles, after a moment's break do the double arm rotation.

## Double Arm Rotation

You need to continue warming up your arms and shoulders. To do the double arm rotation, stand straight with your feet placed shoulder-width apart. As shown, first swing both of your arms upwards (**1**). Now slowly swing your arms behind you (**2**). You finish the double rotation by swinging your arms fully extended to the front (**3**). Repeat this exercise until you have made ten full circles. Increase your rotation speed with the sixth full circle swing.

After a short rest you are ready to go on to exercise another part of your body. You will begin with the toe stand.

## Toe Stand

This exercise will strengthen your legs and help you balance better. The exercise will also strengthen your back. To begin, stand straight with your arms at your sides (**1**). Lift your arms straight in the air and stand on your toes. Hold it, standing on tiptoe for as long as you can, and then return to the original position (**2**). Rest for ten seconds or so and do the exercise again. Try to do it at least five times. After the fifth toe stand, rest a minute and then begin the back stretch.

## Back Stretch

This exercise will continue to loosen up the muscles in your back and shoulders. It will also help your posture. To begin, stand erect and extend your arms straight out in front of you (**1**). Now stretch your arms upwards as high as possible (**2**). Next, bend your body to the front and push your arms backwards as far as possible (**3**). Rest ten seconds and repeat. Try to do the entire exercise five times. Remember to go slowly and **don't** push until it hurts. Pushing an exercise to cause pain can be harm-

2

## Balance Walk

Balancing is an extremely important component of karate. This exercise will help you improve your body balance.

For the balance walk, stand with your left foot directly, heel to toe, in front of your right and extend your arms straight out to each side (**1**). Next, take a step forward, placing your right foot in front (**2**). Keep your arms extended straight out.

1

3

2

ful. Forget the old and inaccurate saying, "No pain, no gain." This is foolish and dangerous.

After you rest for a minute, it's time for the balance walk.

Imagine you are walking on a tightrope and take fifteen to twenty steps. Rest for ten seconds and take another fifteen to twenty steps. Rest again and then do the last fifteen to twenty steps. Be sure to stop and rest briefly between each walk. This is important. Tired muscles cannot be trained for balance.

After a short break, you can sit down and do the toe lifts.

## Toe Lift

You now need to stretch out the muscles in your lower legs. To do the toe lifts, sit on the floor with your legs extended straight out in front of you and bend your head and body forward (**1**). Grasp your toes with your hands and lift your heels off the ground. Hold the position for two seconds (**2**). If you have difficulty reaching your toes, grab your ankles or lower legs and lift your legs slightly. With time you will be flexible enough to grab your toes. Count to five after you drop your foot back to the ground or floor, then do the lift

again. Continue this until you have done a total of five lifts. Strive to increase the time you lift your leg up by the toes from two seconds to three seconds then four, until you can hold your legs up for a full minute. This may take a few months, but it will show you the progress you are making.

You are now ready to get the full body into action. You will do this with the full body bend.

## Full Body Bend

You are continuing to loosen and strengthen the muscles in your body. Full body bends will increase your flexibility. Do these slowly and don't apply too much force. With time and practice you will easily reach the floor. Be careful not to strain your back by trying too hard. If the bend hurts, pull back and don't bend as far forward until you get stronger.

**Step 1** To begin, stand straight with your feet a shoulder-width apart and your hands touching (**1**). Without bending your knees, bend forwards and down to reach as close to the floor as you can. Try to touch the floor. Hold for two seconds, then return to the original position. Take a deep breath and bend down again. Repeat this exercise for a total of five bends (**2**). Rest a minute, then go on to step 2.

**Step 2** You now want to stretch your muscles even more. Just as in step 1, bring your feet closer together as shown (**3**). Do the same move downwards. Again do this slowly. Do a total of five bends. Don't forget to take a deep breath between each bend (**4**). Once you have rested for one minute you are ready to move to step 3.

**Step 1**

1

2

**Step 2**

3

4

(Note: In the beginning, you may need to rest a little longer between each step or cut back to a total of three bends per step.)

**Step 3** This is the most difficult so take your time. It may take you several months before you are able to touch the floor. To begin, place your feet together (**5**). Then, as before, bend forward and downward and try to touch the floor without bending your knees (**6**). Take a deep breath between each bend. Strive to do a total of five bends. Walk around for two minutes and breathe deeply before you go on to the next exercise.

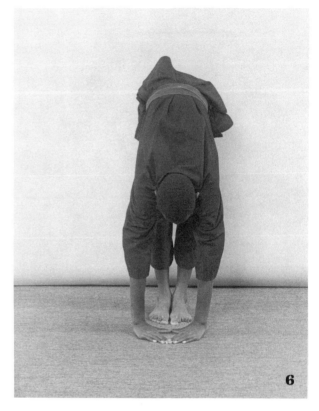

**6**

**Step 3**

**5**

With each step, once you are able to touch the floor easily with your fingertips, try to place your palms flat on the floor. This will allow you to stretch out even more. Try to have patience—you will get there.

Note: Perhaps months from now you can add a step 4 to this warm-up by standing with your feet together and touching your palms to the floor outside your left foot and do the same on the right side without bending your knees. **Warning!** Do **not** attempt to do this until you can complete step 3 easily, touching the palms of your hands to the floor with all five bends.

After a few minutes' walk around the room to relax your muscles, you are ready for the body twist.

## Body Twist

The body twist stretches the muscles of your upper body. Begin slowly with the first four twists. Increase the speed and force with your last six moves to each side. To begin the first twist, extend your arms forward, then twist your body to your left (**1**). Push as far as you can without pain.

Now swing to your right and do the same stretch. Complete the first twist by returning to the front (**2**). Take a deep breath and continue with twist two until you complete all ten twists.

Take a minute's break, then go on to the cross body bend.

## Cross Body Bend

Stand straight and place your feet two shoulder-lengths apart. Keep your legs straight. Bend your left arm and touch your right foot. You may not be able to touch your foot at first, but reach as far as you can (**1**). Come straight up and repeat with the right arm to the left foot. Do a total of twenty of these bends, alternating your left and right arms (**2**). If you want, you can do this exercise before the body twists for a change. After doing the bends, rest for two minutes before you continue. You are now ready for the front leg swings.

## Front Leg Swing

Leg swings will add to your flexibility and balance. This is necessary to help you kick high and with power. To begin this exercise, stand straight with your feet slightly apart (**1**). Next, swing your right leg up to waist height and lower it. Repeat five times with your right leg. Rest a few seconds and do the leg swing five times with your left leg. Try to increase the height of your swing with each repetition. Eventually, you will be able to swing your leg over your head (**2**). As with any exercise, begin slowly and let your ability increase with time and practice.

Rest for a minute before the side leg swing.

## Side Leg Swing

This exercise is especially helpful for building a strong and high side kick. To begin, stand straight with your feet together (**1**). Keep your left leg straight, without bending your knee, and raise it sideways to your belt level (**2**). Try to go a little higher with every swing. Repeat ten times with your left leg and then do the same with your right leg. With each practice session, try to get your legs to go higher.

Rest for one minute and complete the knee jerks.

## Knee Jerk

This exercise will give you greater height in your front kicks. To begin, stand with your right leg behind your left leg (**1**). Jerk your right knee up to your stomach or chest level (**2**) and return to your original position. Repeat this exercise ten times with the right knee and then ten times with the left knee. Go slowly with the first few jerks to avoid pulling any muscles.

Rest a minute and do the deep leg bends.

## Deep Leg Bend

This exercise warms up the muscles on the inside of your legs. Move slowly, and go only as far as you comfortably can. The inside groin muscles are the easiest to strain. Be careful and proceed slowly. To begin, stand with your left leg pushed in front of you, your right leg straight and to your right side (**1**). As illustrated, slowly drop your left knee and begin to lower your weight on that knee. At the same time, lock (do not bend) your right knee and stretch (**2**). This is perhaps the best exercise for your legs and they will help you kick even higher. Repeat this exercise five times to the left, rest for a few seconds, than do five bends to the right. Go directly to the split.

## Split

The split is truly the most difficult exercise to master, especially for boys. This exercise requires good balance and will improve the strength and height of your kicks. To begin, stand with your feet wide apart and knees bent. The left foot is in front (**1**). Very carefully, bend downward and touch the floor with your hands on each side of your front leg as shown (**2**). Slowly move your body downward as you push your back leg rearward and your front leg forward (**3**). Now for the difficult part. *Carefully* stretch until you can't go any further. Repeat the right split, then switch legs to go on to the left side and do it twice on that side also. **Be very careful**. Remember to use your hands for support and don't push too hard. You will feel some tightness in your inner thighs but stop immediately if it becomes painful.

Now rest for two minutes before going to the leg stretch.

## Leg Stretch

Sit down with your right leg behind you and your left leg straight out in front of you (**1**). Bend forward with both hands and try to grab your left ankle. Next, bend forward as far as you can without hurting yourself (**2**). In time you will be able to grab your foot and bring your entire body forward on top of your leg. In the beginning, just try to grab your ankles and work towards grabbing your foot. You can alternate this exercise with the split. Do the split one day and then the leg stretch the next day. Repeat ten times with the left leg and then ten times with the right leg.

Rest for one minute before going to the five-step situp.

## Five-Step Situp

This exercise can be extremely challenging but it will strengthen your abdominal muscles. You need strong abdominal muscles to add strength to your moves and also help guard against kicks and punches to the stomach area. As you complete each step, stop and hold the position for a count of five before moving on to the next step.

Reverse the process by going backwards through step four, three, and so on until you are lying flat back in the first position. Repeat the entire exercise five times. When you are successful in moving through the steps smoothly, without bounces or jerks, you have progressed well.

**Step 1** Lie down on your back with your body flat, your legs together, and your arms locked behind your neck (**1**).

**Step 2** Lift your head and shoulders slightly off the floor (**2**). Hold for five seconds.

**Step 3** Lift your upper back completely off the floor. Keep your feet and legs straight. Do not bend or lift your knees (**3**). Hold for five seconds.

**Step 4** Continue moving forward until you are almost sitting straight up (**4**). Hold for five seconds.

**Step 5** Move forward and bend downward as far as you can and hold for five seconds (**5**).

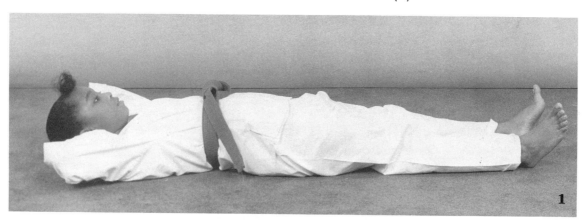

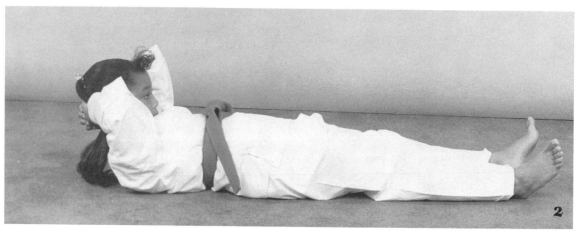

# Partner Exercises

If you have a partner or a colleague from class to practise with you can get a boost in your warm-ups by helping each other. Partner exercises can be used as an occasional alternative to the leg stretching exercises above. However, don't rely on these too much. You need to be able to stretch out on your own.

With a partner, be careful not to push hard. Always release immediately when your partner directs you to stop. The first exercise you and your partner will do is the leg lift.

## Leg Lift

Have your partner lift your leg upwards as you direct. For balance, your partner should gently place one foot on your standing leg and hold your stretching leg under the knee and around the ankle as shown. Repeat this five times with each leg. Start slowly and smoothly and increase your height with time. Change places with your partner. When both of you have finished with the leg lift, go to the leg stretches.

## Leg Stretch

Sit directly in front of your partner. Your partner takes hold of your wrists or arms and places each foot against the inside of your knees (**1**). Next, slowly and carefully, your partner leans back, pulling you forward and thereby stretching your legs (**2**). This is an excellent way to progress faster in your exercises. However, do not be tempted to move too fast. You do not want to strain any muscles. Change places with your partner and go to the body bends.

## Body Bend

Sit down with your legs and feet together. Reach forward slightly and grab your ankles as your partner sits down behind you **(1)**. Together, as you reach forward your partner pushes *lightly* to assist your bend **(2)**. **Be extremely careful with this exercise. Your partner must not push hard or against your lower back**. Change places with your partner and go to the three-way body bends.

## Three-Way Body Bend

Sit down with your legs spread wide apart. Your partner's hands are placed on your shoulders (1). Move your body downward and try to reach your left ankle. Do not bend your knees.

Your partner lightly presses your shoulder downward to assist your bend (2) . . .

. . . Repeat to the right (**3**). As you sit back up, reach both hands and arms forward as far as you can (**4**). **As before, use extreme caution. Do not have your partner push hard or against your lower back.** Change places with your partner.

After you have completed your warm-up exercises you are ready to begin your karate workout. In the beginning, the warm-up exercises will take longer. However, in time you will be able to complete the exercises within thirty minutes. This will allow you about one and one-half hours for your karate workout and the cool-down. For the cool-down exercises, choose three of the warm-up exercises. Choose one that stretches the upper body, one that stretches the legs, and either a body twist or body bend. Finish the cool-down with a slow ten-minute walk.

# Basic Karate Skills

In the last chapter you learned several exercises to prepare you for karate study and practice. You are now ready to learn the basic karate offensive skills of punching, striking, and kicking. First, however, you will learn the stances. Just like any building, the karate student must have a good foundation. Your foundation is your stances.

## The Stances

A strong stance is the most important part of karate. It is your solid foundation. In karate, you will soon discover that you are only as strong as your stance. The strength of a kick or a punch comes from the foundation of the stance. Just as a house cannot stand without a solid foundation, neither can a punch, kick, or block endure without a good stance—the building block of karate. You begin all karate movements from a stance. The first stance for you to learn is the ready, or open, stance.

### Ready Stance

The ready stance, sometimes called the open stance, is the primary stance to use while standing at attention in class or at the beginning and ending of most kata.

Additionally, a trained karate expert can move into any other stance or deliver any kick or punch from the ready stance. You too will be able to move quickly and easily from one stance to another. All it takes is a little practice.

To enter into a ready stance, simply stand comfortably with the feet shoulder-width apart. The knees are slightly relaxed and the fists are held low in front of you. The elbows are slightly bent, each arm looking like a crescent moon (**1**).

Look at this stance from the side (**2**).

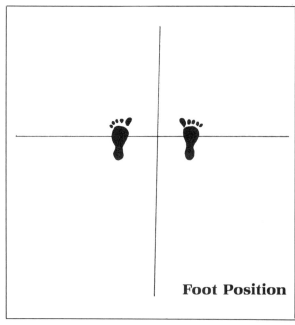

**Foot Position**

Foot Position

## Front Stance

Perhaps the most frequently used stance, the front stance allows you to move to the front or to the rear. Your back leg is kept straight and your knee locked. In the right front stance, your right leg is in front. Bend your right leg at the knee and keep a little more than half of your weight (sixty percent) on it (**1**). To move into a right front stance from a ready stance, shift most of your weight to your left leg. While keeping your hands beside you, slide your right foot and leg out to a forward position. Your back leg remains straight while the right leg is bent at the knee. Note that both feet are facing to the front. To move

1

back into a ready stance, simply reverse the process. Do the opposite for the left front stance (**2**). Notice that your legs are slightly wider than your shoulders and that both feet are pointed straight to the front in both the right and left front stances. You will be able to kick and punch from this stance with great power and balance, so practise both variations daily.

**2**

## Back Stance

The back stance is also a very popular stance. It is the opposite of the front stance. The back stance will seem awkward to you at first and it will be hard for you to balance. In time, however, you will be able to move from a ready stance or a front stance into a back stance with ease. In the right back stance, slide your right leg back and put three-quarters of your body weight on the back leg (**1**). Put the rest of your weight on the left or front leg. Bend both knees slightly. Notice that the backs of both heels are in a straight line. The front foot is pointed straight out in front of you and the back foot is angled 90 de-

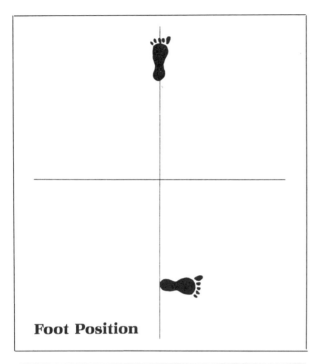

**Foot Position**

grees, or pointed straight off to your right. Your feet should form an L-shape.

To move from a ready stance into a right back stance, shift your weight slightly to the left leg and pull your right leg in close to the left. Then continue to slide your right foot straight back, opening the position of your leg so that your foot points off to the right, or at a right angle to your front leg. In order to get the right balance in the stance, lower your body and shift your weight slightly backwards to "sit lightly" into the stance. Keep your upper body straight. To return to the ready stance, shift your weight forward and reverse your movements. Use the same but opposite procedure for the left back stance (2).

## Cat Stance

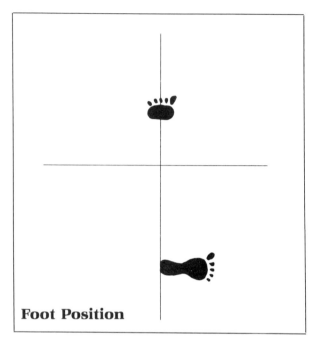

**Foot Position**

Have you ever seen a cat crouching and preparing to attack? You will look the same way as you move into the cat stance. With most of your weight off your back (right) leg, position it in the same manner as you did for the back stance. Then shift all of your weight to your back leg and pull your left leg up close to your body. Lightly touch the floor with the ball of your front foot. To move into a left cat stance from a ready stance, move the left leg forward, then shift almost all your weight (at least ninety percent) onto your back leg while bending the leg deeply. At the same time, move your left foot lightly on the floor with only the ball of the foot touching it, ready to strike. You are now in a left cat stance (**1**). To do a right cat stance, simply switch your legs and repeat the procedure (**2**).

## Horse Stance

Just as you would when riding a horse, you must spread your feet two shoulder-widths apart and bend your knees deeply to do the horse stance. Move your left or right leg to spread your feet wide apart.

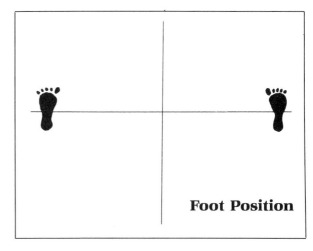

**Foot Position**

Place your body weight equally on both legs and feet. Both knees are deeply bent and both feet are pointing straight forward **(1)**. This stance will be difficult at first, but keep practising and it will become easier. In the horse stance you can use different blocks or attack an opponent with many types of strikes or kicks. It is harder for an opponent to punch or kick you when you are in the horse stance because you become a more narrow target **(2)**. To move into a horse stance from a ready stance, shift your weight and slide one foot outward, taking a large step. The legs must be spread wide, with the knees deeply bent. In the horse stance, the feet are pointed straight ahead with the heels on line as shown in the drawing.

## Closed Stance

bend your knees slightly (**2**). See the drawing for the proper foot position. You will see the closed stance again at the beginning of the katas later in the book.

The closed stance is only used in bowing (**1**), such as to the instructor, or sensei, or an opponent, and at the beginning or ending of a kata. To do the closed stance, move your feet together (actually touching) and

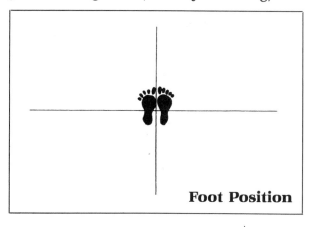

**Foot Position**

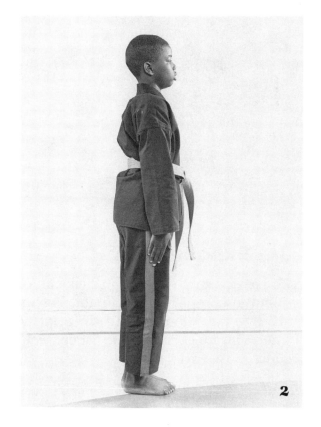

## Offensive Techniques

Now that you have learned the basic foundation of karate, the stances, you are ready to learn how to punch, strike, and kick an attacker or opponent.

## The Punches

The karate punch is used to strike an opponent in competition or an attacker in a self-defense situation. To do a karate punch you must close your fist correctly. Follow these three steps:

**Step 1** Close your fingers tightly at the second knuckle **(1)**.

**Step 2** Roll your fingers into the palm of your hand **(2)**.

**Step 3** Press your thumb over your index and middle fingers **(3)**.

In the beginning, you can remember how to make a fist by using the first word of each step: *close, roll,* and *press.* Soon you will be able to close your fist correctly without thinking about it and use it in a punch.

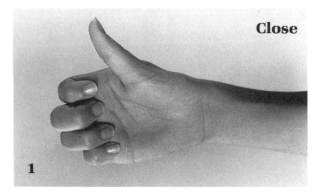

Close

1

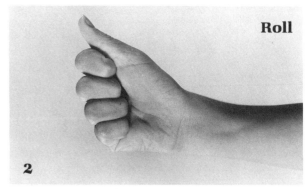

Roll

2

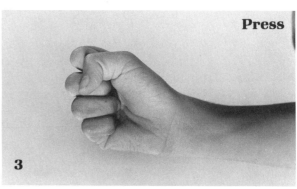

Press

3

## Delivering the Punch

To throw a punch correctly, stand in a ready stance with your right fist held palm upwards at your hip (**1**). This will feel odd at first, but with practice you will soon see how quickly your punches become stronger. Hold your left hand in front with your palm held downward. With your right, punch in a straight line turning your first until the palm faces downwards (**2**). At the same time, pull back your left hand and turn it palm upwards into a fist at your hip (**3**). The first two knuckles of your index and middle fingers are the first to hit the target. Anytime your hand is at your hip palm upwards, you can deliver a punch. By placing your nonpunching hand in front of you, you can deliver a punch with much greater power. This will become natural with practice. Later, instead of just placing your hand in front of you before punching, you will have the hand out blocking or striking before you deliver the punch.

More explanation later.

## Backfist

The backfist is an excellent technique that you can learn quickly. This is an excellent weapon for defense and for sport competition. Stand in a horse stance with your right arm parallel to the floor in front of your chest. Keep your left fist at your hip ready to punch if needed (**1**). Snap your arm out to the side like a whip, extending your elbow (**2**). Immediately upon full extension, return your fist back in front of your chest (**3**). Strike the target using the knuckles of your index and middle fingers (**4**).

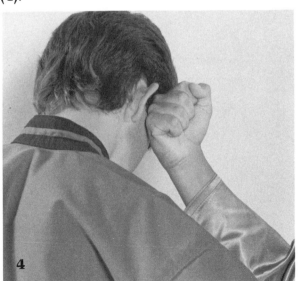

## Knifehand Strike

Known to the public as the karate chop and to karate masters as a shuto (*shoe-toe*), the knifehand is a good technique to learn. As you prepare to move into either a back or cat stance, place your open right hand under your left ear. Cross your left arm in front (**1**). Strike outward with your right hand while turning your right leg to the right. At the same time, pull your left hand back towards your chest (**2**). Keep your

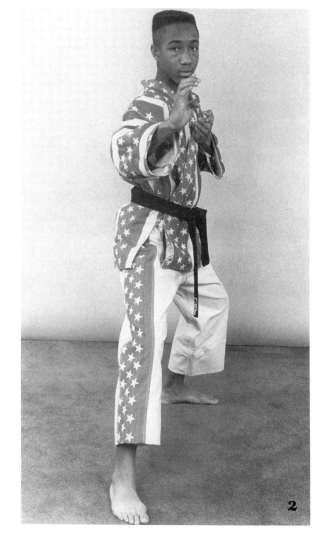

striking hand open with your thumb bent towards the palm. Strike with the outer edge of your hand (**3**). The knifehand strike can be used either as a strike or to block a punch (**4**).

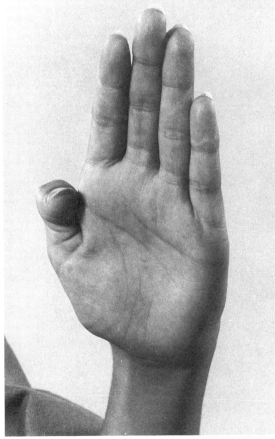

## Power Shuto Strike

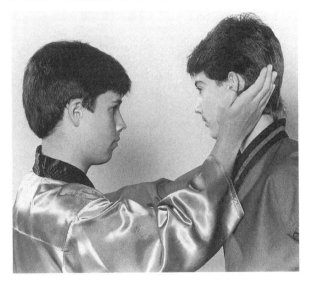

Like the knifehand described above, the power shuto is an open-hand technique that can be an excellent weapon for self defense. The power shuto is not used to block—only as a strike. In a right back stance with your left hand in front for protection, pull the right hand, with fingers fully extended, behind the right side of the head (**1**). With a driving twist, turn your body into a left front stance and extend the hand fully until the target is struck. The nonstriking hand is pulled back to your hip and ready for punching (**2**). As you will learn later, the shuto is in many katas. Exact form is very important to the serious karate student (**3**).

## Ridgehand Strike

Use the ridgehand to strike to the head area of an opponent.

With your left hand in front for protection, swing your right arm and hand as far behind you as possible (**1**). As you be-gin to strike, swing the arm with the elbow extended as you turn your body to the target (**2**). Extend the arm fully to strike the target (**3**). The inside edge of the hand is the striking area. Be sure to tuck your thumb under, away from the striking area (**4**).

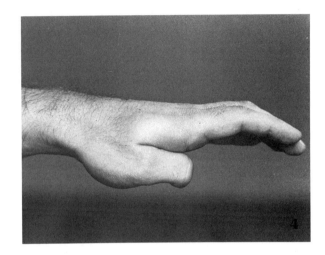

## Reverse Punch

Perhaps the most used punch in kumite today is the reverse punch. It is fast and can be very accurate. Stand in either a back, front, or horse stance. Use your left hand to cover your body in case of an attack. Pull your right hand tightly by your side. Turn your body slightly (**1**). Push the right hand outward while turning the fist upwards (**2**). Extend fully, striking the target with the punch (**3**). Immediately, upon contact, snap the hand back into the original position (**4**).

1

2

3

4

## Palm Heel Strike

The palm heel strike is used to strike the upper face area.

In any stance, pull your right hand back to your chest with the palm facing away from you (**1**). In one quick move, extend the hand outward, striking the target. As you can see, strike with the heel of the palm. Keep your left hand pulled back in a position ready to punch (**2**).

# Elbow Techniques

### Back Elbow

With the back elbow, push your right arm upside down in front of you. Keep your fist closed (**1**). Drive your elbow straight behind you with all of your strength. Keep your arm by your side. Use your left hand to cover your right hand for greater striking power (**2**).

Not really considered a punch, you will see that there are several ways to use the elbow as an offensive weapon. Elbow strikes are not allowed in kumite or sports karate. Be extra careful when you practise these techniques. Elbow strikes are excellent techniques to know for use in life-threatening situations.

The elbow can jab like a knife or strike like a baseball bat.

## Side Elbow

Get into a horse stance. Close your right fist and fold it into your left hand (**1**). Push your right elbow out to the striking area in a jabbing manner (**2**). Just as in the back elbow strike push with all of your strength. If you ever have to use this technique, it is important that you do it with all of your strength.

## Upward Elbow

This is like the uppercut that you may have seen in boxing. Instead of striking with the fist, you use your elbow. Keep your left hand in front of you for protection. In a back stance, place your right hand, opened and at rest, near the center of your chest (**1**). As you move into a horse stance, jerk the elbow straight up, to strike the opponent's chin. In practice, you can strike the palm of your left hand (**2**). This gives you a sense of feeling contact. In combat, the left hand would stay back near your left side, ready for punching.

# The Kicks

You have been introduced to many of the striking techniques that are used with the hands, arms, and fingers. It is now time for you to learn to use your legs and feet offensively. Your legs are nearly three times as strong as your arms. Therefore, your kicks should be three times as strong as your punches. However, balancing while kicking is difficult. You will learn with practice how to shift your weight to one leg and balance when you kick. In this section, you will learn the major karate kicks. These kicks are the front and side snap kicks, the front and side thrust kicks, back kick, roundhouse kick, crescent kick, stomping kick, and the spinning-blade kick.

## Front Snap Kick

Front snap kick is the most basic kick that you will learn. Still it is the favorite kick of many karate masters because it is the most practical. The kick is done with a snapping action of your lower leg.

To kick, stand in a left front stance (**1**). Raise your right knee to waist level. Pull back with your right foot and raise your toes for the kick (**2**). Snap your lower leg forward, locking your knee as you kick (**3**). Then snap your right foot back towards your left knee. Return your foot to its original position (**4**). Do the opposite for a left front kick.

## Front Thrust Kick

1

The front thrust kick is more powerful than the snap kick. It also has a greater reach to strike your target. It differs only from the snap kick in that the heel of the foot is the striking area and you push your kick more into the target.

2

Stand in a left front stance (**1**). Lift your right leg to your left knee (**2**). Pull your body backwards and drive the kick into the target (**3**). Return your foot to the ready position (**4**).

## Side Snap Kick

You can do a side snap kick low, medium, or high. Begin by kicking low and increase your height as you become more flexible.

3

4

Stand in a horse stance (**1**). Pull your hands up in front for protection. Lift your leg so that your foot is about as high as your right knee as shown (**2**). Shift your body to the far right as you raise your knee higher. Kick (in a snapping manner) your left leg to the side, using the edge of your foot to strike the target. Return your left foot above your right knee. Return to a horse stance. Do the opposite for a right side kick (**3**).

## Side Power Kick

You can use a power side kick to strike an opponent's head, chest, or stomach. Start low and as your flexibility increases so will the heights of your kicks.

Stand in a left front stance (**1**). Lift your right leg so that your foot is at your left knee (**2**). Turn your body to the left and extend your right leg straight out, striking

the target with the bottom (heel first) of your foot **(3)**. Pull the leg back and return to your original stance **(4)**. You can do the opposite for a left side power kick.

You can also deliver the kick from the back and horse stances. The strength of this kick comes from the power of all your weight as you spin around and drive your foot outward. The side kick can be thrown with great power. You can easily knock someone three times your size to the ground.

3

4

## Roundhouse Kick

This is a powerful kick to aim at an opponent's stomach, chest, or head. Your body weight is shifted and your balance is very important.

Begin from a right back stance (**1**). Raise your right leg behind your right hip and balance on your left leg. Turn your left knee a little outward (**2**). Swing your right leg in front of your right hip with your

**3**

**4**

**5**

toes pointing up towards the knee **(3)**. Continue the circular motion to the left as you kick your right leg and foot in a snapping motion **(4)**. Strike your target with the ball of your right foot **(5)**. Return your right foot and leg along the same path that you used in delivering the kick. Do the opposite for a left roundhouse kick.

## Back Kick

In a horse stance or ready stance (**1**), bring your right leg up with the knee high in front of you (**2**). With a driving force, kick straight behind you, locking the leg (**3**). Return your leg to the original stance.

This kick is also called a mule kick in that, like a mule, it kicks straight back with great force. Always turn your head and look behind you before the back kick to check the striking area.

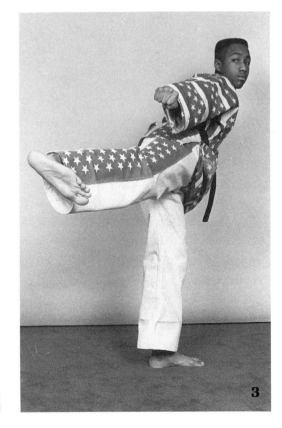

1

2

3

## Spinning Back Kick

Stand in a ready stance or horse stance and shift your weight to your left leg **(1)**. Lift your right leg as high as possible **(2)** and spin your body to the right, rotating

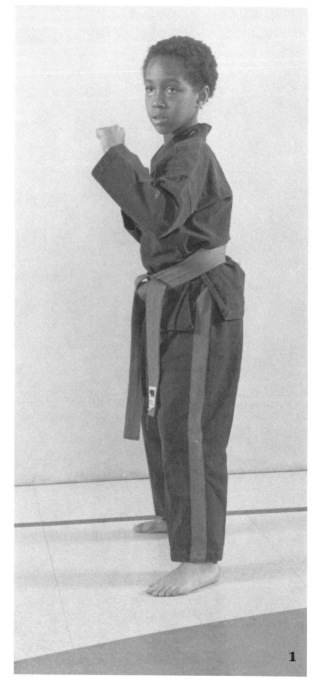

1

Use the spinning back kick to strike an opponent to the head, chest, or stomach. This kick is usually used when an opponent is caught off guard. Always keep your eye on the target.

your weight on your left foot. Push your head forward and extend your right leg directly behind you, striking the target with the bottom of your foot **(3)**.

This is a good kick to use to score a point in a karate match. However, be very careful that you have control of the kick before you try it in a match. You could seriously hurt someone with this kick if you are not extremely careful.

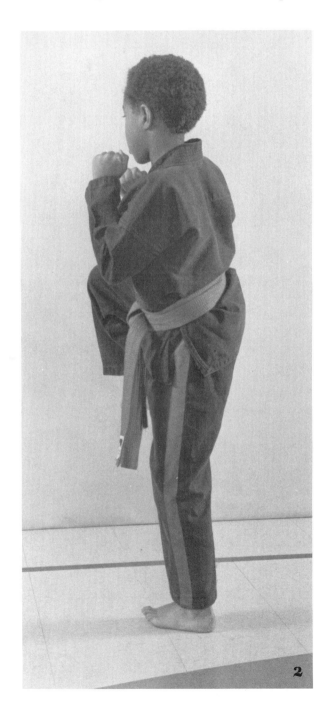

**Spinning Blade Kick**

Use the spinning blade kick against a larger opponent or attacker.

Stand in a left front stance (**1**). Jump into the air off your left leg and spin your body completely around. Keep your right leg high (**2**). As you are in your jump, spin your entire body in the air (**3**). This is very hard to do and takes much practice. Lock your right leg straight out, hitting the target with the side blade or edge of your foot (**4**). Land in your original stance (**5**). Just as in the previous kick, practise this kick until you have great control before you would ever consider using it in a match.

## Front Jump Kick

Use the front jump kick to add extra power to your kick and to gain a greater reach in height for contact. You have probably seen the front jump kick on television or in the movies because it is a dramatic kick.

To do the front jump kick, move into a left front stance (**1**). Jump by shooting your front leg forward and up, bringing your right knee up high (**2**). While in the air, shift your weight and snap out your left leg into a front thrust kick (**3**). Land on your right leg first, then your left leg, to complete the kick.

**1**

**2**

**3**

## Flying Side Kick

You will definitely feel like a Hollywood action star as you learn the flying side kick. Use the flying side kick to give you greater reach in your kicks and to surprise your opponent. It is hard for an opponent to judge your distance while you are in the air.

From a left back stance (**1**), lift your right leg as you begin your jump (**2**). In one movement push hard off your left leg towards your opponent. Keep your feet

together (**3**). In mid-air thrust your right leg and foot out, striking your opponent with the knife-edge side of your foot (**4**). Drop straight down into your original stance. As before, practise this kick until you have great control before using in a match.

## Defensive Techniques

You now have learned many of the major karate punches, strikes, and kicks. It is time to introduce you to the defensive elements of blocking.

## The Blocks

Blocks are just for defense. You deflect or stop your opponent's attack by using blocks. Blocks can be used to block low, medium, and high, inside or outside strikes.

### Low Block

Use the low block to defend against an attack to your stomach or groin area. In a front stance, you can use a low block to deflect a strike or kick to your body. Either

hand can be used in order to effect a block.

Stand in a right front stance. Raise your right fist to the left side of your head. Extend your left hand straight out in front of you in a ready position, palm down (**1**).

1

Bring your right arm downwards and across your chest (**2**). At the same time, pull your left hand back to your waist, palm up. Notice that your right hand is in front and your right leg is forward. Notice that your left hand is ready for punching (**3**).

For a left low block you would do the same series of movements, but from a left front stance.

## High Block

The high block is used to protect your head and face. The same hand and leg are forward for the block. From a right front stance, place your left hand in front and across your chest. Your right fist is at your right hip (**1**). Bring your right arm up across your chest, palm down (**2**). Turn your right arm so your palm faces forward and continue lifting it above your head (**3**). Turn your right arm so your palm faces forward and continue lifting it above your head (**4**). At the same time, pull your left fist back to your hip in a ready position. Do the opposite for a left high block.

## Inside Middle Block

You can use the inside middle block to protect your upper body. In a left front stance, place your left arm across your chest while placing the right arm on the right hip (**1**). Like a coiled spring, snap the left arm upwards to block (**2**). You can do the opposite for a right inside block.

## Outside Middle Block

You can protect your middle and upper body with the outside middle block. From a left front stance, push your right hand forward as you pull your left hand back near your head (**1**). With a swift turn of your body to the right, drive your left arm completely across your body. At the same time, pull your right arm back to your right hip (**2**). Do the opposite for a right outside middle block from a right front stance.

1

2

## X Block

Also known as a cross block, an X block will allow you to stop a strike downwards to the head or a kick to the groin. Get into a horse stance and cross both arms at the chest (**1**). Quickly drive both arms downwards, still crossed, to block a kick (**2**). From the chest, drive the hands upwards and crossed to block a downward strike or hammer blow (**3**).

## Inside Ridgehand Block

The inside ridgehand is specifically designed to block but, like the versatile shuto, the ridgehand can be used for striking also. For a block, in a ready or horse stance, pull your right hand, palm inward, back to your chest (1). Throw your hand

outward to block a punch, using the thumb side of the hand for blocking. Keep the thumb pulled tightly against your hand (2). As stated, the inside ridgehand can also be used as a strike. When striking or blocking with the ridgehand, keep in mind that you are using the opposite side of the hand (3) that you use when you use a shuto or knifehand.

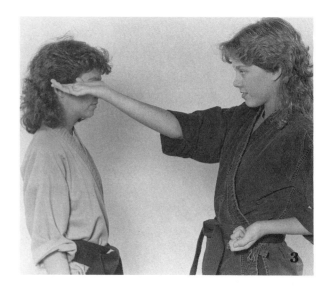

## Crescent Kick

Perhaps the easiest kick in karate can also be used as a block. The crescent kick can be used to block a punch by simply lifting your leg and curving the foot inside (hitting with the inside edge of your foot) **(1)** or outside (hitting with the outside edge of your foot) **(2)**. As you can see, the crescent can be used offensively by striking at the head area **(3)**. This is more of a swinging foot than it is a kick, but it can be quite effective.

You have now been introduced to most of the major blocks used in karate. Go on now to the next chapter and see how you can put all of the elements of karate to practical and artistic use.

# Applying Karate Skills

## Combining Techniques for Self-Defense

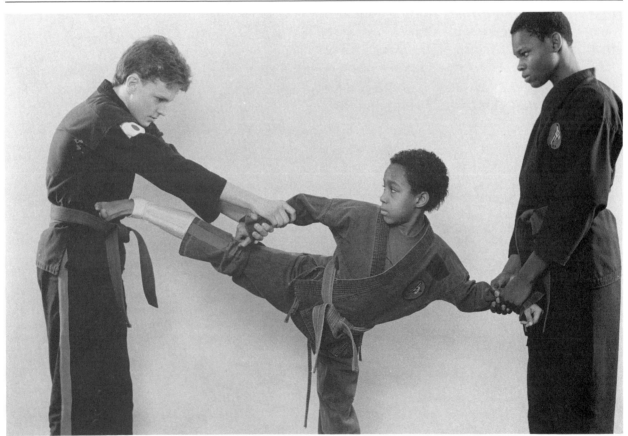

Now it's time to make your karate practice fun and useful. You have been introduced to the stances, punches, strikes, kicks, and blocks. With some thought and coordination, you can combine these moves to defend yourself against an attack. The following sequences show you how to really get into the action. Remember, you do not actually strike your partner. In the beginning, control your strike to within one or two inches of the target. Have fun, but be careful.

## Situation 1

Face your partner in a ready stance. Your opponent stands in a left front stance (**1**) and brings a hammer blow downward towards your head (**2**). To defend yourself, shift into a left front stance. Stop the blow with a left high block (**3**). Now kick your opponent in the stomach with a right front kick (**4**). Follow with a right punch to the stomach (**5**). Practise these moves daily. Repeat this sequence five times. Now try the reverse footing and movements. Your partner stands in a right front stance and strikes at you with a hammer blow. Stop the blow with a right high block. Next, kick your partner in the stomach with a left front kick. Strike him with a left punch to his stomach. Repeat this sequence five times also.

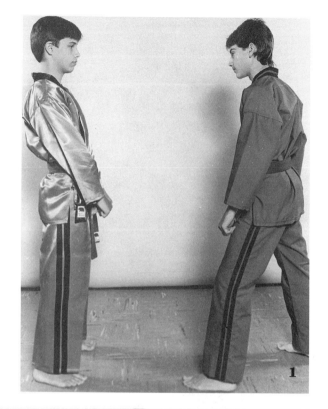

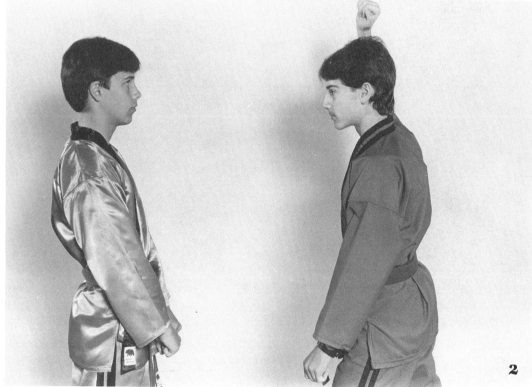

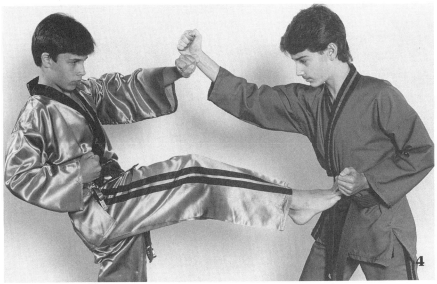

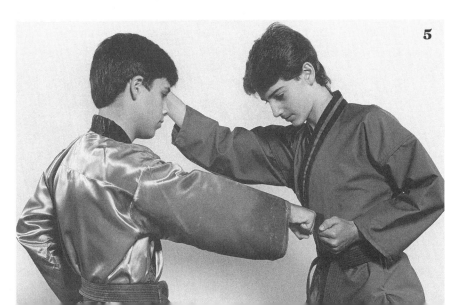

## Situation 2

Face your partner in a ready stance. Your partner stands in a left front stance (**1**) and tries to punch you in the face. Stop the blow with an outside middle block with your right arm (**2**). Lift your right leg so your foot is at your left knee (**3**). Do a right side kick to the stomach (**4**). Step towards your opponent and strike with a right backfist to the head (**5**). Repeat the sequence five times. Again, practise the reverse with the opposite hands and feet. Your partner stands in a right front stance and tries to punch you in the face. Stop the blow with an outside middle block with your left arm. Lift your left leg so your foot is at your right knee. Do a left side kick to the stomach. As before, step towards your opponent and strike, this time with a left backfist to the head. Repeat the sequence to this side five times.

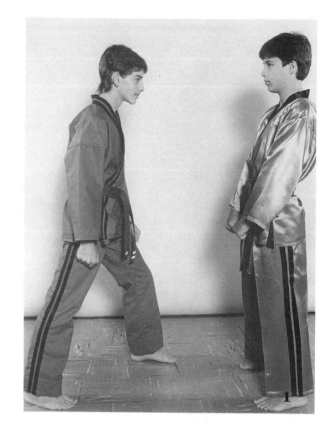

3

4

5

## Situation 3

Face your partner in a ready stance. Your partner stands in a left front stance or a wide ready stance (**1**), then kicks with the right leg to your groin. Block with a left low block as you move into a left front stance (**2**). Step forward into a right front stance while throwing a right punch to the chest (**3**). Repeat the sequence five times. Now reverse the position. In this sequence, your partner kicks with the left leg and you do a right low block as you move into a right front stance. Step forward into a left front stance while throwing a left punch to the chest. Repeat this sequence five times.

As with the above sequences, you need to practise blocking and striking to your left as well as to the right. In the following sequences, do the exercise as illustrated and then practise the same exercise with the opposite side of your body.

## Situation 4

Face your partner in a ready stance. Your partner stands in a left front stance (**1**). Stop your opponent's punch to your chest with an inside middle block with your left arm (**2**). Step forward into a right front stance and do a right knifehand strike to the neck with your right hand (**3**). Repeat to both sides five times each.

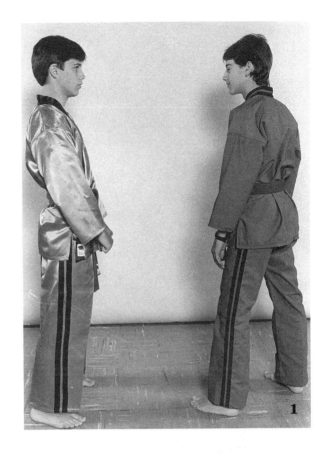

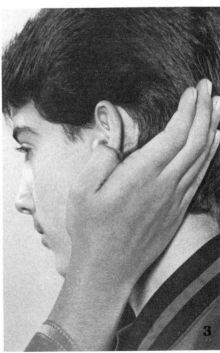

## Situation 5

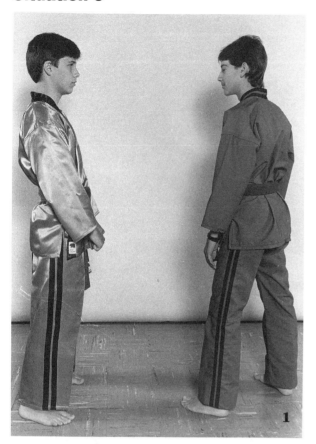

Face your partner in a ready stance. Your partner stands in a ready stance to your side (**1**). Block a front kick to your chest area with an inside middle block with your left arm as you move into a left front stance (**2**). Prepare to deliver a right roundhouse kick at your opponent's head (**3**). Raise your right leg with your foot cocked for the kick (**4**). Snap your right leg for the kick (**5**). Complete the kick to the head (**6**). Repeat to both sides five times each.

## Situation 6

Move left into a horse stance and throw an outside middle block with your left arm to stop the punch (**1**). After the block, throw a left backfist to the attacker's head (**2**). Then move to a right front stance directly in front of the attacker. Aim a left front kick to the stomach (**3**). Return your foot to a left front stance as you move closer to the attacker. Throw a right punch to the attacker's chest (**4**). Finish your move with a left punch to the head (**5**). Do the sequence to both sides five times each.

## Situation 7

Block the attacker's punch with a left inside block as you step back with your right leg into a left front stance (**1**). Quickly throw a right punch to the head (**2**). Finish with a right front kick to the stomach (**3**). Repeat to both sides five times each.

## Situation 8

The attacker's punch is blocked with a right outside center block (**1**). Then grab your opponent's right shoulder (**2**). Pull forward and bend your right knee, striking the chest (**3**). Grab your opponent's

right arm and pull back to your left side as you place your right leg behind your opponent's front leg (**4**). Sweep rearward with your leg, knocking your opponent to the ground. Strike the chest area with a low thrust kick (**5**). Complete this sequence by doing the exercise five times each to both sides.

## Situation 9

You are grabbed around your throat from behind (**1**). Step forward into a right front stance and bring your left arm in front of you (**2**). With all of your strength, drive backwards with a back elbow strike to your attacker's abdomen or chest (**3**). Repeat to both sides, five times each.

## Situation 10

You are grabbed by the throat from the front and choked by an attacker (**1**). Raise your hands high above your head (**2**). Strike down as though you were delivering two lower blocks on the inside of the elbow joints (**3**). Take a step backwards into a left front stance (**4**) and deliver a front snap kick to the attacker's stomach area (**5**). Repeat to both sides, five times each.

## Situation 11

An attacker grabs your arm (**1**). Turn your arm downward and bring your fingers over the attacker's wrist (**2**). Use the attacker's weight to support you and deliver a side snap kick into the chest or stomach area (**3**). Repeat to both sides, five times each.

## Situation 12

You are grabbed by the collar of your shirt or coat (**1**). Use a downward block to break the attacker's hold (**2**). Step back into a front or back stance and prepare to deliver a shuto strike (**3**). Execute the shuto strike to the side of the attacker's neck (**4**). Repeat to both sides, five times each.

## Situation 13

From the front an opponent grabs both of your shoulders **(1)**. Raise both of your arms upwards in high rising blocks **(2)**. Quickly, and with a great snapping action, deliver two shuto strikes to both sides of your attacker's neck **(3)**. Grab the attacker's shirt or coat collar from behind to thrust the head downward at the same time as you are bringing your knee into the chest **(4)**. Repeat to both sides, five times each.

1

2

3

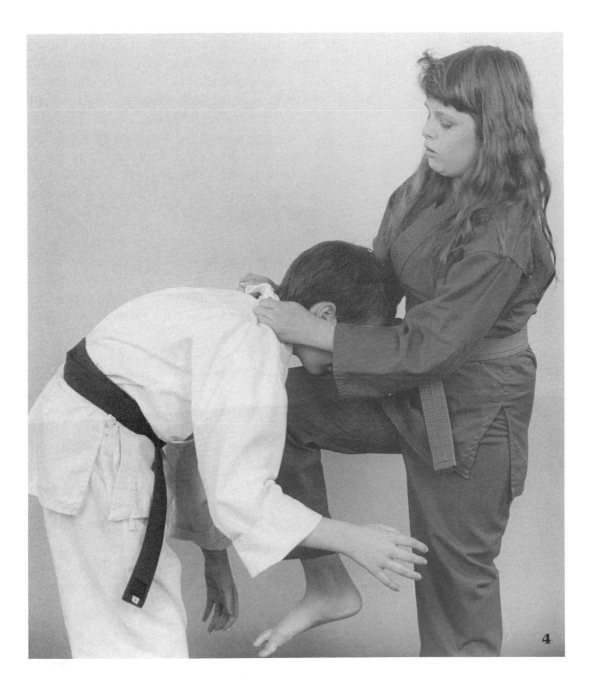

**4**

You can see that there are numerous karate skills that can be combined to give you many self-defense techniques. The above are just a few. With the help of a partner, make up several of your own. Remember to be careful not to actually hit your partner. As you practise many different situations using different combinations of skills, you will soon be able to defend yourself by simply reacting. The karate master never plans in advance what move to use, but simply reacts to each situation. You are now ready to learn about the sport aspect of karate.

## Karate Tournaments

Karate tournaments are held at local, state, regional, national, and international levels all over the world. There is a good chance that at least one tournament is being held annually within a fifty-mile radius of your home. Competition is the heart of sports karate and you will find most tournaments have a welcoming and friendly atmosphere. Karate artists love to make new friends. Although pleasant in spirit, competition is usually tough and extremely demanding. Winners of most tournaments are usually individuals who are serious and devoted students of karate. They practise for long hours daily and enter competitions frequently. Numerous trophies are awarded in several divisions, as determined by age, size, and rank.

Kumite, or free-style sparring, and kata are major elements in both the art and the sport of karate. In time, you will decide whether you want to focus more on karate as an art form, sport, or both.

Tournament karate is usually divided by age, size, sex, and rank. A division for children under six years of age is not uncommon. Often there is a division for five- and six-year-old students. Typically, in kumite, boys compete with boys and girls with girls. In kata competition, boys and girls compete together except in the highest ranks. Size plays an important role in divisions under twelve years of age; after that age a student's rank takes priority. Ideally, age, size, sex, and rank should be equal and well balanced.

## Sparring (Kumite)

When sparring, both you and your opponent are free to kick, strike, or punch each other to score points. Scoring areas are the head (front, side, and back), the body (chest, abdomen and back), and in some tournaments the groin and lower-back, or kidney areas, as shown. Until you have good control, you should avoid striking the lower-back (kidney) or groin areas. Strikes to the throat and neck, vulnerable self-defense targets, should also be avoided. Since you have no idea what your opponent will do, you must be prepared

## Scoring and Major Target Areas

for any kick or punch. Your opponent is a moving target. Both of you will be trying to score. In practice, you can spar as long as you like. However, in a regulation match, such as you might find at a tournament, match time is two minutes or until one of you scores three points. If you score the first three points, you are the winner. If no opponent has three points at the end of the two-minute match, the one

with the most points wins. If neither you nor your opponent have any points, or there is a tie, the match continues until another point is scored. If you score the point, you will be the winner. In order for a point to be scored, a kick, punch, or strike must not be blocked and must be intended for one of the target areas. In tournaments, judges are used and points are awarded by a majority vote of the

judges. There are usually three or five judges including the head referee who co-ordinates the match. Watch for the middle judge to call for a point. The judges award points by raising one hand and pointing with the other to the student who scored. When there is no point, judges cross their arms downwards, as shown. Awards and trophies in the various age and belt level divisions are given for first, second, and third places.

Kumite in the lower belts should be done without actually hitting your opponent. The objective is to stop your kick or punch one inch from the opponent's body or head. However, rules are changing. In many tournaments, light contact to the body is required to score. *Control your kicks and punches. Karate is an art. It was never intended to cause pain except when needed in self-defense, to protect against attack and injury.*

In kumite you will spar several types of opponents. Some of the fighters will be tall and lean (**1**) while others will be short and fast (**2**).

Some fighters are considered "bulls" and hard to move. They like to fight closely and go head to head in the match. These are very powerful fighters (**3**).

Others are "bouncers" who move around the ring quickly. They come in to strike quickly and move rapidly back (**4**). A "charger" is very aggressive, throwing many punches and kicks quickly. You must be very defensive with this type of fighter or you will lose the match to three quick scores (**5**). Still others are defensive fighters, who block kicks and punches from their opponents and strike during openings while under attack (**6**).

## Scoring on Offense

You will begin by practising scoring techniques from an offensive approach. Get into a fighting stance that you feel is the most comfortable. Choose either the cat, horse, back, or front stance. Remember both you and your opponent will be actually moving and, just as in boxing, either

**5**

**4**

**6**

of you can use offensive or defensive moves at any time.

Pretend that you and your partner are in a tournament and practise the following situations. Take turns being the aggressor.

**Situation 1**

Hold your hands high to guard your body and head (**1**). With lightning speed cross over the opponent's block and strike with a left backfist (**2**).

**You have already practised the basic kicks and punches. If you need a refresher, go back and review each punch and kick before you use these in the situations below.**

**Situation 2**
Close in on your opponent and deliver a front punch to the stomach (3). You have to be especially fast to score because this punch can be blocked easily.

3

## Situation 3

Charge your opponent, protecting your-self with your left hand (**4**) and throw a reverse punch to the head of the opponent (**5**). Move out quickly to avoid being hit with a punch or kick.

## Situation 4

Guard your opponent's front hand (**6**) and deliver a front punch to the head (**7**). Again, move in and out quickly.

## Situation 5

From a left front stance, fake a front kick to your opponent's stomach (**8**). Just before you complete the kick, twist your right leg so that it is parallel with the floor (**9**). Continue turning, keeping your knee high, and begin to extend your leg into a right roundhouse kick (**10**). Complete the kick by fully extending the leg and scoring with the roundhouse to the head (**11**). Return your leg to the original position. Once you master the kick, it is very difficult to block.

## Situation 6

From a front stance or back stance throw
a front kick to your opponent's stomach
(**12**). You can use the same kick to the head
area.

**12**

**Situation 7**

From a horse stance, deliver a side kick to the opponent's chest or stomach (13).

13

While sparring offensively, watch for open areas to the head and body of your opponent. Use the above seven situations, but experiment using many combinations of kicks and punches. Use variety on your offense, such as changing from a front stance to a horse stance. Throw combinations of front, side, and roundhouse kicks followed by front punches, backfists, or knifehand strikes.

## Scoring on Defense

Many students prefer to fight defensively. They like to block an opponent's advance and score with a countermove.

### Situation 1

Your opponent throws a punch to your head. You block with a middle block (**1**). Counter with a front kick to the stomach (**2**).

## Situation 2
Block your opponent's backfist (**3**).
Counter with a punch to the head (**4**).

## Situation 3

Block your opponent's backfist (**5**). Strike
with a knifehand to the neck (**6**).

## Situation 4

In this situation, your opponent charges in with a jumping front punch. Lower your body and block with a rising upper block (**7**). Score with a reverse punch with the right hand to the body (**8**).

## Situation 5

Your opponent delivers a front kick to your body. Block the kick with a lower block (**9**). This turns your opponent around (**10**) to where you can score with a punch. Use either a punch to the body or to the head (**11**).

## Situation 6

Block your opponent's front kick with a left lower block (12). Set your hand for a left backfist (13). Quickly strike with the backfist to the head for the score (14).

12

13

14

### Situation 7

In this situation, your opponent delivers a front right punch to your head **(15)**. As you block with a right middle block, score with a left punch to the head **(16)**.

## Situation 8

In this situation you try to fake your opponent out by throwing a fake backfist **(17)**. As your opponent raises an arm to block, throw a fast front kick to the stomach **(18)**. Or, you might want to follow the fake with a right roundhouse kick to the head **(19)**.

# Karate Forms (Katas)

Karate forms have been called the most important part of karate. In kata, you use planned moves that look almost like ballet or dance. Kata is really the *art* of karate, and the movements can be beautiful and quite graceful. Most importantly, katas allow you to practise your blocks, kicks, strikes, and punches in a formal pattern of movements.

Most advanced katas look like the movements of an animal such as a cat, a tiger, or a snake. Looking down at a kata from overhead, the pattern will look like a letter of the alphabet, such as H, T, or K, or a plus sign (+). Katas have a name, a number, or both. The first kata here is called Heian (*he-on*) One. You follow an H-form pattern in this and all heian katas. Heian Two is in my book, *Total Karate*, also published by Sterling, so Heian Three follows Heian One here. There are hundreds of katas. Form and power are the most important things in these katas. The katas are not done fast. Each move is paced on a "one-thousand-one, one-thousand-two" count. Judging is based upon correctness of form. Usually there are three or five judges who call out their scoring of the kata between one and ten. Ten is a perfect score.

# Heian One

Stand in a closed stance as you announce your kata. Pretend you are facing the judges. Bow (**1**).

Bring up your right leg, cross your arms and breathe in deeply (**2**).

Step down into an open stance with fists tightly closed and your arms extending down in front (**3**).

Move to your left at 90 degrees and do a lower left block in a left front stance (**4**).

Step forward into a right front stance as you deliver a right front punch to the chest level **(5)**.

Turn 180 degrees to your right and deliver a right downward block **(6)**.

Pull your arm in as you sweep with your right foot. Rotate your wrist and swing your fist to your face and circle outward (**7**).

Complete the circle with a hammer strike (**8**).

Step up and deliver a left punch to the chest level as you move into a left front stance **(9)**.

Turn to face the judges straight ahead. Deliver a low block with the left hand in a left forward stance **(10)**.

Pull your arm inward and shift three-quarters of your weight onto your back leg (**11**).

Immediately snap your left arm into an upward rising block. Pretend to grab the arm (**12**).

Step forward and deliver a rising block **(13)**.

Step forward and block again with a left rising block. Grab the arm **(14)**.

Step forward into a right stance with a breaking block. Remember to tuck the hand upside down, resting on your hip when it is not blocking or punching (**15**).

Turn your body to the far left (**16**) and move into a left lower block in a left front stance (**17**).

Deliver a right front punch in a right front stance (**18**).

Begin your turn to the right, and do a right lower block in a right front stance (**19**).

Step up in a left front stance and do a left center punch (**20**).

In the next step, turn to your left and do a left lower block in a left front stance. Your back is now to the judges (**21**).

With the judges behind you, you have just completed a lower left block in a left stance (**22**).

Begin to step up with a right punch **(23)**.
Complete the punch from a right front stance **(24)**.

Again prepare to step up and punch with the left hand (**25**).

Complete the punch in a left front stance (**26**).

Prepare to step up and punch with the right hand. Complete the right punch in a right front stance (**27**).

Now turn to the left by bringing your right leg far around behind your body (**28**).

Spin into a right back stance and deliver a knifehand strike with the left hand. You are now facing the judges again **(29)**.

Step up and place your feet together with your left knifehand in front and the right hand prepared at your left ear **(30)**.

29

30

Step out into a 45 degree angle to the left in a left back stance while striking with a right knifehand (**31**).

Swing your body to the right and place your left knifehand in front and draw your right hand, palm inward, to your left ear (**32**).

Deliver a right knifehand in a left back stance straight ahead **(33)**.

Place your left foot close to your right and bring your left hand, palm inward, to your right ear **(34)**.

Deliver a left knifehand strike 45 degrees to the right in a right back stance **(35)**.

Pull your left hand and left foot back and face the judges. Bow **(36).**

# Heian Three

This second Heian kata also follows the H-form pattern. In fact, all of the Heian katas have an H-form pattern.

Bow to the judges (**1**).

Lift up your right leg, cross your arms and breathe (**2**).

You are now ready to begin the kata **(3)**.

Turn to your left and do a short right back stance and inside center block **(4)**.

Step up into a closed stance with feet together and at the same time do a left lower block and right outside center block **(5)**.

Snap the arms back in a breaking motion into a left inside center block and a right lower block **(6)**.

Turn 180 degrees to your right and do an inside center block with your right arm while in a short left back stance (**7**).

As before, step into a closed stance and do a left center block and a right lower block at the same time (**8**).

In a breaking motion, change the blocks to a left lower block and a right inside center block (**9**).

Turn back to the center (facing the judges) and do a left lower block in a left front stance (**10**).

Move your right foot over your left and prepare to do a complete 180 degree turn (**11**).

Move completely into a wide ready stance and place your fists up against your sides (**12**).

Push both hands outward and pull both feet together into a closed stance (**13**). Your back is to the judges.

Pull both arms tightly and place your hands upside down in punching positions by your sides (**14**).

Lift your right leg up and prepare to do
a crescent kick block (**15**).

Swing your right leg and block a punch
(**16** front view).

Set your right leg down into a horse stance and move your elbow to the left to block another punch **(17)**.

Snap out with a right backfist **(18)**.

17

18

Now bring the left leg over, using it as a crescent block **(19)**.

Block with the elbow **(20)**.

Do a backfist strike **(21)**.

Remember to always bring the backfist strike back to the original position **(22)**.

Still moving in a straight line, do a crescent block with the right leg (**23**).

Elbow block (**24**).

Backfist strike **(25)**.

Reach back out with the right hand and pretend to grab your opponent **(26)**.

Step up and punch with your left hand
in a closed stance (27).
Pull your left foot around (28) . . .

Continue to swing around and pull your left arm back to elbow strike behind you **(29)** as you prepare to move into a horse stance.

Complete the move by striking rearward with the elbow as the right hand punches behind your head **(30)**. These last moves **(28–30)** are done quickly, in one swift action. You are now in a horse stance.

Do the same position by shifting your arms to the other side, with a little hopping motion in the horse stance. Now the right arm elbows and the left hand punches (**31**).

Cross your arms and bring your feet together (**32**).

Bow (**33**).

31

32

**33**

Practise these katas daily. Learn some new katas as well. Try to improve your form and power as you do the katas. Take your time and go slowly. Do not increase your speed until you can do the katas with gracefulness and balance. Katas are considered by many instructors to be a large part of karate. Katas are also used to grade rank. The higher the rank, the faster and stronger the kata. Katas also increase in difficulty as you move up in rank.

Practise daily and try to find a qualified instructor in your town. Please remember to always be careful and never strike an opponent or attacker unless your life is in danger.

# Advanced Techniques

After you have studied karate for a few years, you may be introduced to advanced techniques such as fighting multiple attackers or using karate weapons.

Here are examples of what you may someday be able to do:

## Situation 1

Two attackers grab you by each arm (**1**).

1

You lift up your right leg and kick the first attacker with a side kick. You remember to use the heel and knife edge of your foot **(2)**. Then you lift up the arms of your other attacker and deliver a front kick to the stomach or chest **(3)**.

## Situation 2

Two attackers grab your arms and a third begins to choke you (**1**). Immediately, you kick the individual in front of you in the stomach or groin (**2**). Setting your foot back down, you then lift and throw a right side kick to the attacker on your right (**3**).

1

Now you turn and kick your last attacker from the groin area (**4**). As he bends over from pain, you turn and grab him by the arm with both of your hands and force him to the ground (**5**). You turn and make your escape (**6**).

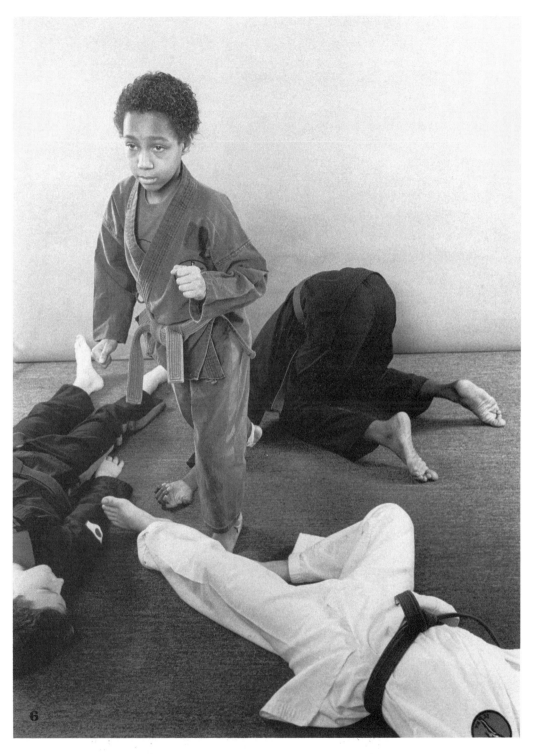

These and other advanced techniques should be taught by an instructor once you have learned the basics well. It is something to work towards. Until then, always be very careful using karate.

Weapons are not really part of karate. Some martial arts weapons used in karate were actually fashioned in Okinawa from farm tools at a time when weapons of any type were outlawed under martial law.

You do not have to study karate to learn how to use martial arts weaponry. However, karate masters learned quickly that these simple weapons could be an extension of "the empty hand" and soon mastered the techniques. While no instruction is provided here, it is important to note that such weapons can easily hurt or kill an opponent with little effort. Never practise with these weapons without the direct supervision of a qualified instructor. Three of the most popular karate weapons are the nunchaku (**1**), the bo, or bo staff (**2**),

2

1

and the tonfa (**3**). Of historical interest, the original use of the nunchaku was to take the shell off of rice. The bo could have been the wood part of a hoe while the tonfa came from the handles of the wooden plow. One of the oldest weapons, found in the Orient hundreds, perhaps, thousands of years ago, is now a common toy, the yo-yo.

As you can see there is much to learn about karate. The great masters of yesterday made change upon change and those of today continue to examine and experiment with how the body can be used as a weapon for self-defense. And now you can be a part of it.

Good luck in your study of this wonderful and beautiful art we call karate.

# INDEX

# ABOUT THE AUTHOR

**J. Allen Queen** was born in Lincoln County, North Carolina, and graduated from West Lincoln High School in 1969. He earned a B.S. and an M.A. degree, both in Elementary Education, at Western Carolina University, completing the doctoral program in education at the University of Virginia in 1978.

Presently a professor in the School of Education at the University of North Carolina at Charlotte, Dr. Queen has served as a Principal in the Charlotte-Mecklenburg Schools, as Principal with Kings Mountain Schools, as Chairman of the Department of Education at Gardner-Webb College, and as a classroom teacher.

J. Allen Queen's interest in karate is long-standing; he has studied karate for over twenty-five years and has been an instructor for close to twenty years. Holder of a fifth-degree black belt, he currently teaches karate only in seminars and special classes.

Queen is the author of five books on karate, all specifically written for elementary and junior-high school students. His works have been published in the United States, Canada, Europe, and Australia.

Dr. Queen, his wife, Patsy, and their son, Alexander, currently live in Kings Mountain, North Carolina.